THE FINAL RESTING PLACE

Calvary Cemetery

EDWARD BONNER

an imprint of Sunbury Press, Inc.
Mechanicsburg, PA USA

LOCAL HISTORY PRESS

an imprint of Sunbury Press, Inc.
Mechanicsburg, PA USA

Copyright © 2024 by Edward Bonner.
Cover Copyright © 2024 by Sunbury Press, Inc.

Sunbury Press supports copyright. Copyright fuels creativity, encourages diverse voices, promotes free speech, and creates a vibrant culture. Thank you for buying an authorized edition of this book and for complying with copyright laws. Except for the quotation of short passages for the purpose of criticism and review, no part of this publication may be reproduced, scanned, or distributed in any form without permission. You are supporting writers and allowing Sunbury Press to continue to publish books for every reader. For information contact Sunbury Press, Inc., Subsidiary Rights Dept., PO Box 548, Boiling Springs, PA 17007 USA or legal@sunburypress.com.

For information about special discounts for bulk purchases, please contact Sunbury Press Orders Dept. at (855) 338-8359 or orders@sunburypress.com.

To request one of our authors for speaking engagements or book signings, please contact Sunbury Press Publicity Dept. at publicity@sunburypress.com.

FIRST LOCAL HISTORY PRESS EDITION: October 2024

Set in Adobe Garamond Pro | Interior design by Crystal Devine | Cover by Lawrence Knorr | Edited by Debra Reynolds.

Publisher's Cataloging-in-Publication Data
Names: Bonner, Edward, author.
Title: The final resting place : Calvary Cemetery / Edward Bonner.
Description: First trade paperback edition. | Mechanicsburg, PA : Local History Press, 2024.
Summary: The road to a tender heart is through the Calvary Cemetery. This final resting place concludes the journey for these beautiful souls. This writing is a masterpiece of history transcribed by pen onto paper.
Identifiers: ISBN : 979-8-88819-232-0 (paperback).
Subjects: HISTORY / Military / General | HISTORY / General | SPORTS & RECREATION / General.

Designed in the USA
0 1 1 2 3 5 8 13 21 34 55

For the Love of Books!

For all the people buried at the Calvary Cemetery
and to all the souls in the world.

CONTENTS

1	Introduction
11	Richard Caliguiri
14	Billy Conn
17	David L. Lawrence
20	Harry A. Stuhldreher
22	Harry Greb
24	Norman Frauenheim
26	Frank Gorshin
28	Biddle Brothers
32	Bob O'Connor
34	Patrick J. Sullivan
35	Jimmy "Greenfield" Smith
37	Michael J. Muldowney
38	Wallace "Bucky Williams
40	Matthew "Gene" Lyons
41	James "Pud" Galvin
43	Mary Lou Williams
46	Bishop Vincent Leonard
48	Bill Regan
50	Julius Joseph "Moose" Solters
52	Herb Drury
54	Joseph A. McArdle
55	John B. "Jack" Butler
57	Patricia Dobler
59	Rev. James R. Cox
61	Gregory Ignatius Zhatkovich

64	Enos Kirkpatrick
66	James M. Morin
68	James Francis Burke
70	John Kane
73	Gerald Anthony Bucciarelli
75	John J. Kane
76	Judge Walter R. Little
77	Anthony Fagnelli
80	William J. Coyne
82	István (Stephen) Kerekes
84	Local Burials
86	Our Babies
91	Infant New Section
93	Religious Sisters
96	Clergy
97	The Forgotten
100	The Legends, the Heroes
104	76th PA Infantry
106	155th PA Infantry
108	Independence Day
109	The Pauper Graves
110	Light Shining Down
115	Random Beauty
136	Calvary Cemetery Map
137	Biddle Newspaper Article
141	Placing Flags for Memorial Day
144	Acknowledgments
145	About the Author

INTRODUCTION

Calvary Catholic Cemetery is located at 718 Hazelwood Avenue in the Greenfield and Hazelwood neighborhoods of Pittsburgh, Pennsylvania, USA. It was established on November 6, 1886, by the Reverend Richard Phelan, President; James Phelan, Vice President; Judge Chas. F. McKenna; J. Dawson Callery; John D. Scully; John Burns; Rev. Thos. Devlin; John Kelly; Anthony F. Keating; Jas. J. Flannery; and the Diocese of Pittsburgh. The entire number incorporated thirty-two people. The first interment was made in June 1888. More than 150,000 interments and entombments have taken place at Calvary Cemetery.

The cemetery includes several tracts of land that were bought at different times. The original purchase was the Jones farm, 101.17 acres, bought from John M. Tiernan, who had foreclosed on a mortgage on the farm. The date of purchase was June 21, 1886. Later, the cemetery purchased additional land from the Alta Vista Land Company.

As an entrance was needed on Hazelwood Avenue, 2.2 acres were purchased on July 18, 1887, from John Keyser. The lot had a frontage of 105 feet on Hazelwood Avenue and extended back from this street for about the same distance; it was bought on March 5, 1900, from James H. Costello. A driveway from Hazelwood Avenue to the cemetery was opened.

Calvary Cemetery remains the largest of the diocesan cemeteries. Today, it includes two beautiful chapel mausoleums, an extensive garden crypt development, the exclusive Cardinal Wright Oratory crypts, a large priests' plot, and Shepherd's Rest, a mausoleum set aside for the burial of bishops of the Diocese of Pittsburgh.

Many notable and not-so-notable people are buried at the Calvary Cemetery. I have gathered information to present you with a formal, short history of each individual.

Year 1872

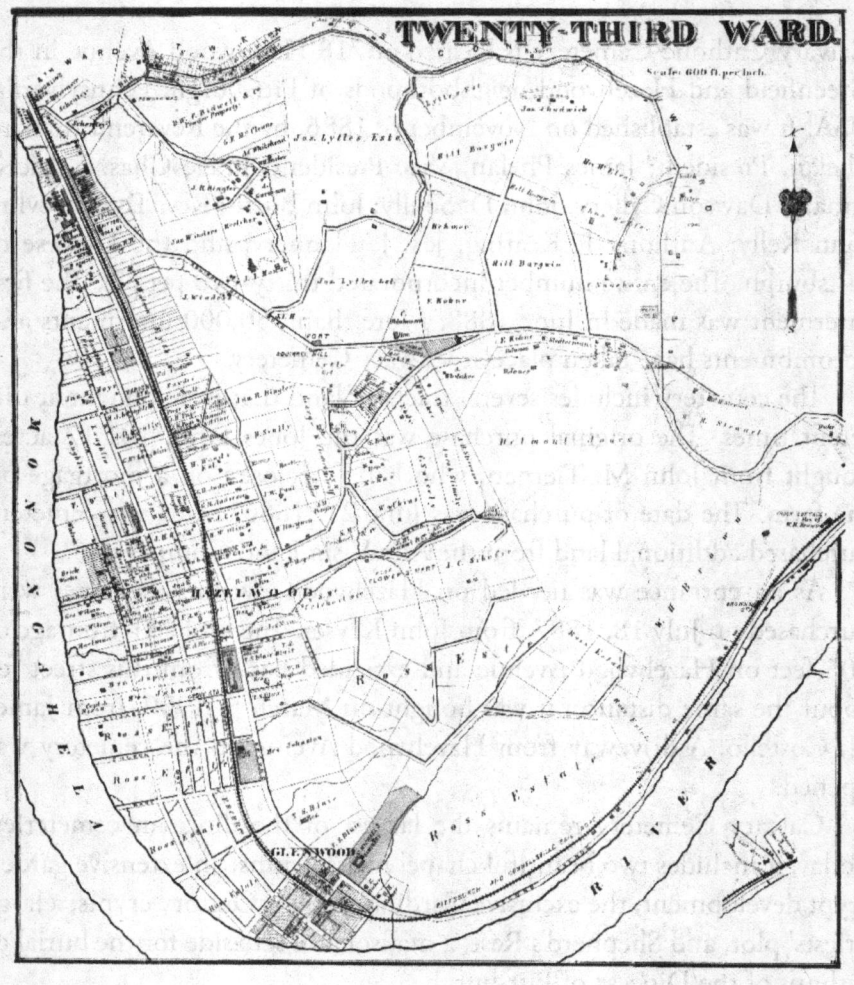

CALVARY
CEMETERY
1888

The Final Resting Place

Introduction 7

The Final Resting Place

The Final Resting Place

RICHARD CALIGUIRI

Born October 20, 1931, Richard S. Caliguiri was of Italian Albanian descent and grew up in Pittsburgh's Greenfield section. After graduating from Taylor Allderdice High School in 1950, Caliguiri won his first mayoral seat in 1977.

During the collapse of the steel mills in Pittsburgh, Richard Caliguiri reshaped the city of Pittsburgh, calling it "Renaissance Two." During his term in office, the likable mayor oversaw the development of One Oxford Center, PPG Place, and the BNY Mellon building. He established the longstanding Great Race and the Pittsburgh Marathon.

Mr. Caliguiri listened to the people and addressed the varied problems in the city's neighborhoods. In 1986, in response to some citizen complaints and legal action by the ACLU, by order of Mayor Caliguiri, the city placed a plaque entitled "Salute to Liberty." It read:

> During this holiday season, the City of Pittsburgh salutes liberty.
> Let these festive lights remind us that we are the keepers of
> the flame of liberty and our legacy of freedom.

Three years later, by two 5-4 decisions, the United States Supreme Court upheld in part and denied in part the city's position in the County of Allegheny v. American Civil Liberties Union [492 US 573 (1989)]. The American Civil Liberties Union challenged two public-sponsored holiday displays in Pittsburgh. The first involved a Christian nativity display inside the Allegheny County Courthouse. The second display was a large Hanukah menorah erected yearly by the Jewish organization outside the City-County building. The ACLU claimed the displays constituted state endorsement of religion. This case was decided with Chabad v. ACLU and City of Pittsburgh v. ACLU of Greater Pittsburgh.

The conclusion was a 5-to-4 decision; the court held that the scene inside the courthouse unmistakably endorsed Christianity in violation of the Established Clause. By displaying the words "Glory to God for

Richard Caliguiri

the birth of Jesus Christ," the county clearly stated that it supported and promoted the Christian doctrine. The court also held that not all religious celebrations on government property violated the Clause. Six of the justices concluded that the display involving the menorah was constitutionally legitimate, given its setting.

After his first term, Caliguiri was diagnosed with Amyloidosis, a rare disease that occurs when an abnormal protein called amyloid builds up in the organs and interferes with their function. Despite his condition, he continued to serve the city of Pittsburgh.

In 1988, Richard Caliguiri passed away from the disease at 55 years of age. The people of Pittsburgh loved his leadership and mourned his passing. In October 1990, a commemorative statue of Caliguiri sculpted by Robert Berks was dedicated on the steps of the Downtown Pittsburgh City-County Building on Grant Street.

BILLY CONN

THE 1946 CONN—Heavyweight Contender Billy Conn sends a right ripping into the heavy bag as he opens his training camp at Greenwood Lake, New Jersey. Billy's date with Louis is June 19—at $100 per look!
—(Associated Press Wirephoto.)

 Known as "The Pittsburgh Kid," Billy Conn was the World Light Heavyweight Champion from 1939 to 1941. Billy was an Irish American boxer from East Liberty. He debuted as a professional boxer on July 20, 1934, against Johnny Lewis. Billy Conn knocked out Johnny Lewis in the third round.
 Conn built a record of 47 wins, nine losses, and one draw (tie), with seven knockout wins, before challenging for the World Light Heavyweight title. Along the way, he beat former or future world champions Fritzie Zivic, Solly Krieger, and Fred Apostoli, as well as Teddy Yarosz and Young Corbett III. He won the world light heavyweight championship

Billy Conn

Billy Conn and Joe Louis

against Melio Bettina on July 15, 1939, at Madison Square Garden. Later that same year, on September 25, Bettina lost another unanimous decision to Conn at Pittsburgh's Forbes Field.

In 1941, Billy Conn gave up his light heavyweight title to challenge Joe Louis, the World Heavyweight Champion. On June 18, 1941, in New York City, Conn fought Joe Louis. Louis outweighed Billy by more than 25 pounds at ring time. After 12 rounds, Billy was ahead on two scorecards and even on one. He wobbled Joe Louis in the 12th round, and in the 13th, Billy Conn went for the knockout.

Billy had a big smile on his face. "This is easy," he said. "I can take this sonuvabitch out this round."

His trainer cried out, "No, no, Billy! Stick and run. You got this fight won. Stay away, kiddo. Just stick and run, stick and run."

And then it happened. Billy tried to pound Joe Louis, but Louis managed the violent burst, then penetrated a monster on the challenger's jaw. Billy Conn got knocked out with only 2 seconds left in the 13th round.

In 1998, Ring Magazine ranked the fight 6th greatest title fight in history.

DAVID L. LAWRENCE

David L. Lawrence was the 37th Governor of Pennsylvania from 1959 to 1963. He also served four terms as Pittsburgh's Mayor, from 1946 through 1959. As mayor, David Lawrence directed the nation's first urban renewal program for Pittsburgh. "Renaissance One" saw the smoke control industry's completion, the Point's transformation into the Gateway Center, and the development of Mellon Square.

During his four-year term as governor, Lawrence endorsed historic preservation, expanded the library system, and passed anti-discrimination legislation, environmental protection laws, and Pennsylvania's Fair Housing Law. He also passed rigorous highway safety legislation, which some attribute to the death of two of his sons in an automobile accident. His expansion came at the price of budget deficits and tax increases, a move that angered many fiscal conservatives.

Governor David L. Lawrence, upon hearing that Senator John F. Kennedy carried all 32 Pennsylvania electoral votes in the 1960 presidential race, displays victory sign at Democratic headquarters here 11/8. (Pittsburgh, PA, UPI Telephoto)

In early life, Lawrence was too poor to attend college. Instead, he worked as a clerk for Pittsburgh attorney William Brennan, the chairman of the local Democratic party and a labor movement pioneer. Brennan became a personal friend and mentor to the teenage Lawrence.

Lawrence entered the insurance business in 1916. In 1918, he enlisted in the United States Army to aid the United States effort in World War I, serving as an officer in the adjutant general's office in Washington, DC.

When he returned home from his army service in 1919, Lawrence was elected chairman of the Allegheny County Democratic Party. At that time, Pittsburgh was a Republican power base, and the Democrats held broad support only in the lower class and among recent immigrants, who were concentrated in industrial jobs. With the help of Joe Guffey, a future Pennsylvania Senator, Lawrence led the rising Pennsylvania Democratic party that would soon dominate local and statewide politics. Limited to one term under existing state law, Lawrence retired from office in 1963. He continued to be active in Democratic politics and was chairman of the Kennedy and Johnson administrations.

Lawrence and his wife, Alyce, had five children, three boys and two girls. Their eldest son was named Brennen in honor of William Brennen's role in getting Lawrence started on a lifelong political career.

On April 19, 1942, Lawrence and his wife were having dinner with their friends at the Pittsburgh Athletic Club. Brennen, 16, went joyriding with some of his Central Catholic High School classmates and took David Jr., 13, along for the ride. The boys all played on the same baseball team.

State Police said the 19-year-old driver had lost control of the Lawrence family car. While passing other vehicles, his car skidded off the road and went backward, hitting a tree along Route 19 in Zelienople. Brennen was killed instantly, and David Jr. was rushed to Ellwood City Hospital but died en route. The other five boys in the car survived with multiple injuries.

Lawrence's remaining son, Gerald Lawrence, became the longtime vice president and general manager of Churchill Downs, the prominent racetrack in Louisville, Kentucky.

Lawrence's grandson, Tom Donahoe, served as General Manager for the Pittsburgh Steelers from 1991 until 1999. He helped the team to Super Bowl XXX. He later served as GM for the Buffalo Bills from 2001 until 2005 and contributed to ESPN.com.

On November 4, 1966, David Lawrence fell ill and collapsed at a campaign rally held at Pittsburgh's Syria Mosque for gubernatorial candidate Milton Shapp. He was rushed to a local hospital, where he died 17 days later. He was 77 years old.

Many buildings were named in honor of Lawrence, including the David L. Lawrence Convention Center in Pittsburgh and the David Lawrence Hall of the University of Pittsburgh.

HARRY A. STUHLDREHER

Harry Stuhldreher was born October 14, 1901, in Massillon, Ohio. He grew up there and delivered papers with Luther Emery, the legendary Massillon sportswriter. Harry had a three-year football career at Massillon High School. He was described as a good but not outstanding player. In 1920, Harry moved to Pennsylvania, where he played football for Kiski Prep and graduated in 1921.

Harry A. Stuhldreher played quarterback at the University of Notre Dame from 1922 to 1924. He was a three-time all-American and a member of the famous Four Horsemen. Harry played for Notre Dame's legendary coach, Knute Rockne, in 1922, 1923, and 1924. Notre Dame's record during his three years was 29-2-1, and his team captured the National Championship in 1924 with an undefeated record of 10-0. Stuhldreher was a leader who not only could throw accurately but also returned punts and proved a solid blocker. He was one of the most undersized quarterbacks in Notre Dame history, standing at 5'7" and 151 pounds. Mr. Stuhldreher was selected virtually unanimously as the All-American quarterback.

After graduating from Notre Dame, Stuhldreher played professional football with the Brooklyn Horsemen/Lions in 1926. He served as head coach at Villanova from 1925 to 1935 and head coach and athletic director of the University of Wisconsin-Madison from 1936 to 1948.

Leaving Wisconsin, Stuhldreher joined US Steel in Pittsburgh in 1950. He died in 1965 in Pittsburgh of acute pancreatitis.

Harry Stuhldreher

His college record as a coach was 110 wins, 87 losses, and 15 ties. In 1958, he was inducted into the College Hall of Fame as a player for Notre Dame.

HARRY GREB

Edward Henry "Harry" Greb (June 6, 1894 – October 22, 1926) was an American professional boxer. Nicknamed "The Pittsburgh Windmill," "The Smoke City Wildcat," and "The Pittsburgh Bearcat," Harry Greb was regarded by boxing historians as one of the best pound-for-pound boxers of all time. He was the American Light Heavyweight champion from 1922 to 1923 and the World Middleweight champion from 1923 to 1926. Greb fought 298 times in his 13-year career, combining 108 wins, 49 knockouts, 8 losses, and 3 draws.

Harry Greb had excellent stamina and constantly threw punches from all directions. He was also considered a dirty fighter, using elbows, thumbs, and his head as often as his fists. Most of Greb's reputation for being a dirty fighter comes from the sensationalized and myth-filled book by James Fair, *Give Him to the Angels*. This work is so full of exaggerations and outright lies that it was pulled from the shelves after only one printing due to threats of lawsuits by Greb's family.

Regardless, the damage was done; the falsehoods in the book were committed to memory and passed down to succeeding generations of fight fans who had nowhere else to go to get information on the late boxer.

Many opponents said that Greb was more rough than dirty. His boxing tactics had no set style that a competitor could anticipate, and no pattern could be studied to learn his techniques and gain an edge in fighting him.

Greb is the only man who defeated Gene Tunney in 1922 for the vacant American Light Heavyweight title. Tunney, who beat Greb in four later matches, went on to dethrone heavyweight champion Jack Dempsey in 1926.

Having been thumbed in the eye by an early opponent, Greb lost sight in one of his eyes. Over the last third of his career, the sight in his good eye declined rapidly, ultimately forcing him to retire at 32.

In September 1926, Greb had a significant operation, having his right eye removed and replaced with a glass eye. On October 22, 1926, Greb checked into an Atlantic City Hospital for surgery to repair a damaged nose and respiratory tract caused by years of boxing. At 2:30 p.m., Greb passed away from complications during the operation two months after retiring.

NORMAN FRAUENHEIM

Norman Frauenheim was an American pianist and music teacher. He was acclaimed for his performances in America and Europe for many decades. His many students also remember him for bestowing the style of his famous teachers and for outstanding guidance with their repertoire. Born in Pittsburgh, Pennsylvania, on October 29, 1897, Norman Frauenheim was the fifth of the seven children of Edward J. and Antoinette Marie "Nettie" Vilsack Frauenheim, whose parents co-founded the Pittsburgh Brewing Company.

Norman Frauenheim attended Shady Side Academy in Pittsburgh and Fordham University. He served briefly in the United States Navy in World War I. He studied music in Paris in the 1920s and, afterward, studied with Ignacy Jan Paderewski. He was also a student of Zygmunt Stojowski for many years. Frauenheim made concert tours in France, Spain, and Great Britain. His American debut was in 1926 at Town Hall, New York City. He was a soloist with the National Symphony Orchestra under the direction of Antonia Brica, the first American female conductor. He performed in New York City and Pittsburgh from the late 1920s to the late 1930s. Around 1940, Frauenheim moved to Washington, DC, where he continued to perform until 1960.

In 1946, Frauenheim performed at Carnegie Hall in Midtown Manhattan in New York City. He taught privately in New York City and Pittsburgh and was a music professor at the Carnegie Institute of Technology (now Carnegie Mellon University.) For four decades, he was a well-known piano teacher in the Washington metropolitan area. In 1955, he married Enid Mitchell, an English countess. They had no children. Unfortunately, she died early in the marriage. A year before his death, around 1988, Norman Frauenheim moved back to Pittsburgh. He died at the age of ninety-two. As of 2021, his estate is valued at an estimated ten million dollars.

FRANK GORSHIN

Frank John Gorshin Jr. (The Riddler) was born in Pittsburgh, Pennsylvania, on April 5, 1933. Frank Gorshin was an American character actor, impressionist, and comedian. He had many guest appearances on *The Ed Sullivan Show* and *Tonight Starring Steve Allen*. His most famous star role was The Riddler on the live-action television series *Batman*. His performance launched the character to become a significant villain against Batman.

Gorshin was of Slovenian ancestry. His father, Frank Sr., a second-generation Slovenian American, was employed as a railroad worker. Frank Jr.'s mother, Frances, used to work as a seamstress. She had come to the United States as a young girl from Lower Carniola, Slovenia.

At age fifteen, Frank Gorshin Jr. got a part-time job as an usher at the Sheridan Square Theater in Pittsburgh. During his employment at the theater, Frank Jr. memorized movie stars' behavior and gestures, creating his impressionist gig. In 1951, while attending Peabody High School, Gorshin won a talent contest in Pittsburgh. His prize was a one-week paid engagement at Jackie Hellier's New York nightclub, The Carousel. After graduating high school, he attended Carnegie-Mellon Tech School of Drama. He acted in plays and performed in nightclubs during his spare time.

In 1953, at nineteen, he was drafted into the US Army and was stationed in Germany. Frank served for two years as an entertainer attached to Special Services. In the Army, Frank met Maurice A. Bergman, who introduced Frank to a Hollywood agent when his term in the service ended. In 1956, Frank landed a role in *The Proud and Profane*, a dramatic war romance by William Perlberg-George Seaton Productions.

In 1957, Frank was visiting his relatives in Pittsburgh. While he was enjoying his family, his agent called him to rush back to Hollywood to audition for a movie called *Run Silent, Run Deep*. Instead of flying, Frank drove his car to Los Angeles, California. After going for over thirty hours, Frank fell asleep at the wheel and crashed his car. He suffered a fractured skull and fell into a coma for four days before waking in the hospital. He recovered and starred as The Riddler, for which he received an Emmy Award nomination, as well as in many "B" movies.

Gorshin died at seventy-two in Burbank, California, on May 17, 2005. He had lung cancer, emphysema, and pneumonia.

JACK BIDDLE AND ED BIDDLE

Born in Essex County, Ontario, Canada, Jack (January 8, 1872) and Ed (December 27, 1876) Biddle arrived in Pittsburgh having already embraced a life of crime. Known as the leaders of the "Chloroform Gang," they would overpower their victims with chloroform before robbing them. On April 12, 1901, their unethical character led them to a Mount Washington household of a wealthy grocer. The brothers' robbery turned to manslaughter when the grocer discovered them in his home. Local detectives tracked the Biddle boys down but lost one of their number, Pat Fitzgerald, who was shot in a gunfight. Once apprehended, Jack and Ed were charged with murder and sentenced to death by hanging.

During their months of imprisonment, the Biddle brothers and other County prisoners began to receive visits from the wife of the jail's prison warden. Kate Dietrich Soffel ministered to the county's prisoners under the authority of her husband, Peter Soffel. Through their interactions, Kate Soffel became captivated with Ed Biddle. The extent of her affection was portrayed by the tools she purposely hid under her coat to ease the Biddle brothers' escape. While the brothers sawed the bars and

concealed the cuts with black wax, the men and their cells were occasionally searched, but nothing suspicious was found.

On January 30, 1902, Mrs. Soffel chloroformed her husband, dressed in her best clothes, and sat up all night waiting for the right time. With Mrs. Soffel's help, the Biddle brothers broke out of the county jail and headed northward by trolley towards West View. Once they reached the end of the line, Kate and the Biddle boys stole a horse and sleigh from a local farm. Armed with a stolen gun, the escapees headed to Canada. Because of the January cold, Kate and the Biddles stopped at the Stevenson's Hotel on Butler Plank Road. Staying approximately four hours at the hotel, the escapees again took to the snow-covered road.

The Biddle boys and Mrs. Soffel traveled nine more miles on their escape route before detective Charles "Buck" McGovern and his posse caught up to the escapees, who had made a pit stop at the Graham family farm. Clashes between the two groups erupted in gunfire, and this resulted in the fatal wounding of both Jack and Ed Biddle.

Jack Biddle died at the Butler Hospital at 7:30 p.m. on February 1, 1902; Ed Biddle died three hours later. Jack was 28 years old, and Edward was 24 years old. The bodies were taken to the morgue in Pittsburgh,

where they were on exhibition for some hours and were then turned over to their brother, Harry Biddle, who took them to an undertaker's room in the South Side. They were buried at the Calvary Cemetery.

Mrs. Soffel was shot and survived the injury. It was said that either she shot herself or made Ed Biddle shoot her. Mrs. Soffel was prosecuted for her part in the jailbreak and sent to the State Prison for two years. Her husband divorced her and moved the children to Ohio. After her release, Kate Soffel tried her hand at the theatrical business. She performed the role of her association with the Biddle Brothers. Authorities stopped the performance. She went into seclusion, changed her name, and earned her living as a dressmaker. It was said she was fully repentant for her infatuation with Ed Biddle.

Kate Soffel

On August 30, 1909, she died at the West Pennsylvania Hospital in Pittsburgh from typhoid fever. Kate Soffel was cremated on August 31, 1909, and her ashes were deposited privately in her mother's unmarked grave at the Smithfield East End Cemetery on September 1, 1909.

The office of the last Deputy Warden of the old Pittsburgh jail was the location of Mrs. Soffel's bedroom. The Deputy Warden said: "I'm not a believer in the spirit world, but some creepy things happened." A picture on the wall moved on its own; he heard sand shifting in the walls, and he felt a cold hand on his arm that he believed was that of Mrs. Kate Soffel. Prisoners at the Allegheny County Jail complained about seeing the ghosts of Ed and John Biddle roaming the halls.

BOB O'CONNOR

Robert E. O'Connor Jr. (December 9, 1944 – September 1, 2006) was an American politician who was the Mayor of Pittsburgh from January 3, 2006 until his death. Known as "The People's Mayor," O'Connor's down-to-earth personality and easygoing attitude made him famous.

His "Redd Up Pittsburgh" campaign was born out of his distaste for litter, which he often called disrespectful to Pittsburgh; it became a massive success.

Born in the Greenfield neighborhood and a longtime resident of Squirrel Hill, O'Connor graduated from Pittsburgh's Taylor Allderdice High School in 1962 and was inducted into their alumni hall of fame in 2011. He worked briefly as a steelworker and then entered the restaurant business. He eventually became executive vice president of the Pappan chain of restaurants in Pittsburgh.

First elected in 1991, Bob O'Connor served on the city council under Mayors Masloff and Murphy. Elected as City Council President in 1998, he soon resigned to serve in the administration of Pennsylvania Governor Ed Rendell.

When Mayor Tom Murphy chose not to seek a fourth term, O'Connor returned to Pittsburgh and won the election with 67% of the vote.

After seven months in office, Mayor O'Connor was diagnosed with a rare brain cancer. Yarone Zober, recently appointed Deputy Mayor, served as acting mayor during his treatments. Mayor O'Connor passed away on September 1, 2006. The Bob O'Connor Golf Course at Schenley Park was named in his honor.

Along with O'Connor's wife, the O'Connors' three children also attended the ceremony: Father Terry O'Connor, a priest from Munhall who also gave the blessing; daughter Heidy O'Connor Garth; and Pittsburgh City Councilor Corey O'Connor.

"The one word that comes out when I think of my dad is unselfish. He just had a beautiful heart," said Father O'Connor. Later, Heidy O'Connor Garth told the crowd: "Do what my dad would do: Be kind to others, pay it forward, and above all, love Pittsburgh."

PATRICK J. SULLIVAN

Patrick Joseph Sullivan was a Republican member of the US House of Representatives for Pennsylvania. Born in Pittsburgh, Pennsylvania, on October 12, 1877, Sullivan worked in the Homestead Axle Works from 1890 to 1900 and in the steel mills in Pittsburgh from 1900 to 1909.

He was a member of the city council from 1906 to 1909 and served as an alderman from 1910 to 1929, police magistrate from 1916 to 1923, and a member of the board of assessment and tax revision for Allegheny County, Pennsylvania, from 1923 to 1929.

Patrick J. Sullivan was elected as a Republican to the Seventy-first and Seventy-second Congresses (March 4, 1929-March 3, 1933). He was unsuccessful as a candidate for renomination in 1932. He was the city police magistrate in Pittsburgh from 1936 until his death on December 31, 1946.

JIMMY "GREENFIELD" SMITH

James Lawrence Smith was a Major League Baseball infielder known as "Jimmy Greenfield Smith" or "Bluejacket." Jimmy's parents were James Smith, who emigrated from Edinburgh, Scotland, and Katherine (O'Donnell) Smith, who emigrated from Wales. James Smith worked as a blacksmith at the J & L Steel Mill in Pittsburgh, Pennsylvania. He and Katherine had six children: Margaret, Helen, Jimmy, Katherine, Mary, and Thomas.

Jimmy Greenfield Smith was born May 15, 1895, in Pittsburgh and raised in the Greenfield section of town. In April 1913, Jimmy began his baseball career playing for Duquesne University. During the summer, Jimmy played in a semi-pro league in St. Mary's, Ohio. Known as a heavy hitter, Jimmy signed a professional contract with the Chicago Whales club during the latter part of the season in 1914.

Smith was a switch hitter and threw right-handed. Jimmy's major league debut with the Chicago Chi-Feds was on September 26, 1914.

In February 1916, Jimmy Smith signed with the Pittsburgh Pirates. Known as fast as lightning and a great fielder, Smith was thought to replace the aging Honus Wagner.

During some rough times, the Pirates released Jimmy in August. He signed with the New York Giants and played thirty-six games, hitting a .229 average. The Giants went on to win the World Series pennant that season against the Chicago White Sox.

In February of 1918, the Giants sold Jimmy to Boston. He was used as a utility player, hitting a .225 batting average.

In February of 1919, Jimmy was traded to the Cincinnati Reds. That year, the Reds won the World Series, where Jimmy's only gameplay was as a pinch hitter in Game 7. Playing with various teams, Jimmy's final game was with the Philadelphia Phillies on September 3, 1922.

During Prohibition, Jimmy bootlegged alcohol from many cities into his Greenfield neighborhood. Jimmy was also the father-in-law to Billy Conn, the world light heavyweight champion.

MICHAEL J. MULDOWNEY

Born August 10, 1889, in Philadelphia, Philadelphia County, Pa., Muldowney graduated from Duquesne University in 1908 and became a deputy sheriff for Allegheny County. Muldowney was elected as a Republican to the Pennsylvania House of Representatives for the 1925 term and was reelected to serve two more consecutive terms. Muldowney was elected council for Pittsburgh (1930–1933); elected to United States Congress (1933–1935), then had an unsuccessful campaign for reelection. He was appointed to the State Board of Mercantile Appraisers (1935–1937), and appointed referee to the State Unemployment Compensation Board (1940–1947). Michael J. Muldowney died March 30, 1947, in Pittsburgh, Allegheny County, Pennsylvania.

WALLACE "BUCKY" WILLIAMS

Wallace "Bucky" Williams was a Negro League baseball player, and at the time of his death, he was the second-oldest living former Negro League player behind 104-year-old Emilio Navarro. Williams was a team member for the Pittsburgh Crawfords (1927–1932) and Homestead Grays in 1936. He was known to play earlier with the sandlot Pittsburgh Monarchs. A lifetime .340 hitter, Williams played third base and shortstop. Bucky played with great players such as Leroy "Satchel" Paige, Josh Gibson, Oscar Charleston, and Buck O'Neil. Bucky was saddened by the fact that very few young people know much about the Negro Leagues. Williams also umpired in the East End Little League Association for several years, where his son, David, played. He was a guest during Pittsburgh Pirates games at PNC Park and occasionally connected with players he competed against.

Williams was born in Baltimore, Maryland, and was the son of Joseph and Mathilda Williams. At the age of six months, his family moved to Pittsburgh and joined St. Charles Lwanga Parish in Pittsburgh's East End. His wife, Marjorie, whom he married in 1936, died in 1976. After his baseball playing days, Williams worked with the Edgar Thomson Steel Works of US Steel in Braddock, Pennsylvania.

He is an honorary member of the Negro League Hall of Fame, and in 1995, he traveled to Kansas City for a gathering with the old-time league players. To celebrate his 100th birthday, a party was held on December 16, 2006, at the Churchill Country Club.

Williams died one month before his 103rd birthday, November 16, 2009. Highmark Square project at PNC Park produced life-size bronze statues of Pittsburgh Negro League greats: Wallace "Bucky" Williams, catcher Josh Gibson of the Homestead Grays and Pittsburgh Crawfords, Crawford's pitcher Satchel Paige, Crawfords/Grays outfielder Cool Papa Bell, Grays/Crawfords center fielder-manager Oscar Charleston, Grays first baseman Buck Leonard, Grays/Crawford's infielder Judy Johnson and Grays pitcher Smokey Joe Williams.

MATTHEW "GENE" LYONS

Gene Lyons was a television actor from Pittsburgh, known for his role as police commissioner Dennis Randall on the NBC series *Ironside*, starring Raymond Burr.

Gene, a life member of the Actors Studio, was in the Broadway production of *Witness for the Prosecution*. His other Broadway credits include *This Rock*, *Harriet*, *Death of a Salesman*, *An Enemy of the People*, *The Trip to Bountiful*, and *Masquerade*.

Before joining Raymond Burr as a regular on *Ironside*, Gene appeared on *Perry Mason* in 1965 as murderer Ralph Balfour in "The Case of the Wrathful Wraith." He also made guest appearances on two dozen television programs.

Gene Lyons had two known relationships: with Grace Kelly and Lee Grant.

Lyons died in Los Angeles, California, on July 8, 1974, from complications related to alcoholism.

JAMES "PUD" GALVIN

James Francis "Pud" Galvin (December 25, 1856 – March 7, 1902) was an American Major League Baseball pitcher in the 19th century. He was MLB's first 300-game winner in 1888 and was inducted into the Baseball Hall of Fame in 1965.

His nickname "Pud" originates from when Galvin made hitters look like pudding when he pitched. Other nicknames he was given were "The Little Steam Engine" because of his size and "Gentle Jeems" because of his kind disposition.

Galvin grew up in Kerry Patch, St. Louis, Missouri. His baseball debut was for St. Louis of the National Association in 1875. He played for various teams and leagues. On August 20, 1880, he was the first major league pitcher to throw a no-hitter on the road, leading his team, the Buffalo Bisons, to a 1-0 victory over the Worcester Worcesters.

Galvin was traded to the Pittsburgh Alleghenys during the mid-season in 1885. He played for the Pittsburgh club from 1885 to 1889, pitching over 300 innings yearly. He went to the Pittsburgh Burghers of the Players League, then returned to the Alleghenys (now the Pittsburgh Pirates.)

Galvin played in a two-person pitching rotation, so he pitched 6,003 innings and played 646 games. Both recorded totals came second to Cy Young's.

Galvin died poor at age 45 on March 7, 1902, in Pittsburgh, Pennsylvania. A Roman Catholic, Galvin was buried in the Calvary Cemetery.

In 2006, on a Nation Public Radio station broadcast, Galvin was cited as a widely known user of a performance-enhancing substance called Brown-Sequard elixir, which contained monkey testosterone. No one seemed bothered by the use of the elixir in Galvin's day, and the news media practically endorsed it by saying it was "the best proof yet furnished for the value of the discovery."

MARY LOU WILLIAMS

Mary Lou Williams (born Mary Elfrieda Scruggs; May 8, 1910 – May 28, 1981) was an American jazz pianist, arranger, and composer. She wrote hundreds of compositions and arrangements and recorded more than one hundred records (in 78, 45, and LP versions). Williams wrote and arranged for Duke Ellington and Benny Goodman, and she was a mentor and teacher to Thelonious Monk, Charlie Parker, Miles Davis, Tadd Dameron, Bud Powell, and Dizzy Gillespie.

In 1922, at twelve, she went on the Orpheum Circuit of theaters. The following year, she played with Duke Ellington and his early small band, the Washingtonians. One morning at three o'clock, she played with McKinney's Cotton Pickers at Harlem's Rhythm Club. Louis Armstrong entered the room and paused to listen to her. Williams said, "Louis picked me up and kissed me."

In 1927, Williams married saxophonist John Overton Williams. She met him at a performance in Cleveland, where he was leading his group, the Syncopators, and moved with him to Memphis, Tennessee. He assembled a band in Memphis, which included Williams on piano. In 1929, 19-year-old Williams assumed leadership of the Memphis band when her husband accepted an invitation to join Andy Kirk's band "Twelve Clouds of Joy" in Oklahoma City. Later, Williams joined her husband in Oklahoma City but did not play with the band.

Mary Lou was one of the greatest jazz pianists, composers, and arrangers ever. Williams was a swing and bebop icon. "The Lady Who Swings the Band" also devoted herself to aiding musicians in need and teaching younger generations about jazz's rich African American heritage.

The group, Andy Kirk's Twelve Clouds of Joy, moved to Tulsa, Oklahoma, where Williams was employed transporting bodies for an undertaker when she was not working as a musician. Williams joined her husband when the Clouds of Joy accepted a longstanding engagement in Kansas City, Missouri. He began sitting in with the band and serving as its arranger and composer. She provided Kirk with such songs as "Froggy Bottom," "Walkin' and Swingin'," "Little Joe from Chicago," "Roll 'Em," and "Mary's Idea."

In 1942, Williams, who then divorced her husband, left the Twelve Clouds of Joy and returned to Pittsburgh. She was joined there by bandmate Harold "Shorty" Baker, with whom she formed a six-piece ensemble. After an engagement in Cleveland, Baker left to join Duke Ellington's orchestra. Williams joined Duke Ellington's orchestra in New York City, then traveled to Baltimore, where she and Baker were married.

She left Baker and the group within a year and returned to New York. Williams accepted a job at the Café Society Downtown, started a weekly radio show called Mary Lou Williams's Piano Workshop on WNEW, and began mentoring and collaborating with younger musicians.

In 1952, Williams accepted an offer to perform in England and stayed in Europe for two years. By this time, music had taken over her life, and not in a good way; Williams was mentally and physically

drained. A three-year hiatus from performing began when she suddenly backed away from performing shows in Paris. She returned to the United States and converted to Catholicism, along with Dizzy Gillespie's wife Lorraine, in 1954.

Father Peter O'Brien, a Catholic priest, became her close friend and manager in the 1960s. Dizzy Gillespie introduced Williams to Pittsburgh's Bishop John Wright. Bishop Wright let her teach at Seton High School on the city's North Side. There, she wrote her first Mass, called "The Pittsburgh Mass." Williams eventually became the first jazz composer commissioned by the church to compose liturgical music in jazz.

In 1981, Mary Lou Williams died of bladder cancer in Durham, North Carolina, at the age of seventy-one. Dizzy Gillespie, Benny Goodman, and Andy Kirk attended her funeral at the Church of St. Ignatius Loyola. She was buried in the Calvary Catholic Cemetery in Pittsburgh.

BISHOP VINCENT LEONARD

Vincent Martin Leonard (December 11, 1908 – August 28, 1994) served as Bishop of Pittsburgh from 1969 to 1983.

Leonard was born in Pittsburgh, Pennsylvania, and was one of nine children of Francis and Catherine (née Dolan) Leonard. His father, Francis, worked in the steel mills to feed the family. Leonard was raised in the Hill District neighborhood of Pittsburgh and received his early education at the parochial school of St. Brigid Church. After graduating from Duquesne University Preparatory School, he studied at Duquesne University in Pittsburgh and then at St. Vincent Seminary in Latrobe.

Bishop Hugh C. Boyle ordained Leonard to the priesthood on June 16, 1935. His first assignment was as assistant chaplain at Mercy Hospital, where he remained for two years. From 1937 to 1950, he was resident chaplain of Allegheny County Home and Woodville State Hospital. He was later named assistant chancellor (1950), chancellor (1951), and vicar general (1959) of the Diocese of Pittsburgh.

In addition to these duties, he was pastor of St. Patrick Church in the Strip District (1955–1967) and St. Philip Church in Crafton (1967–1969). He was named a domestic prelate by Pope Pius XII in 1952.

On February 28, 1964, Pope Paul VI appointed Leonard as Auxiliary Bishop of Pittsburgh. The following April 21, he received his episcopal consecration from Bishop John Wright. After Bishop Wright was named to head the Congregation for the Clergy, Leonard was appointed the ninth Bishop of Pittsburgh on June 1, 1969.

He became one of the first bishops in the United States to make his diocesan financial reports public during his tenure. He established a due process system to allow Catholics to appeal any administrative decision they believed violated canon law. In 1974, he threatened three priests with disciplinary action for giving Communion in the hand when it was not yet permitted in the United States.

Leonard resigned as Bishop of Pittsburgh on June 30, 1983, due to arthritis. He later died from pneumonia at the Little Sisters of the Poor Home in Pittsburgh at age 85.

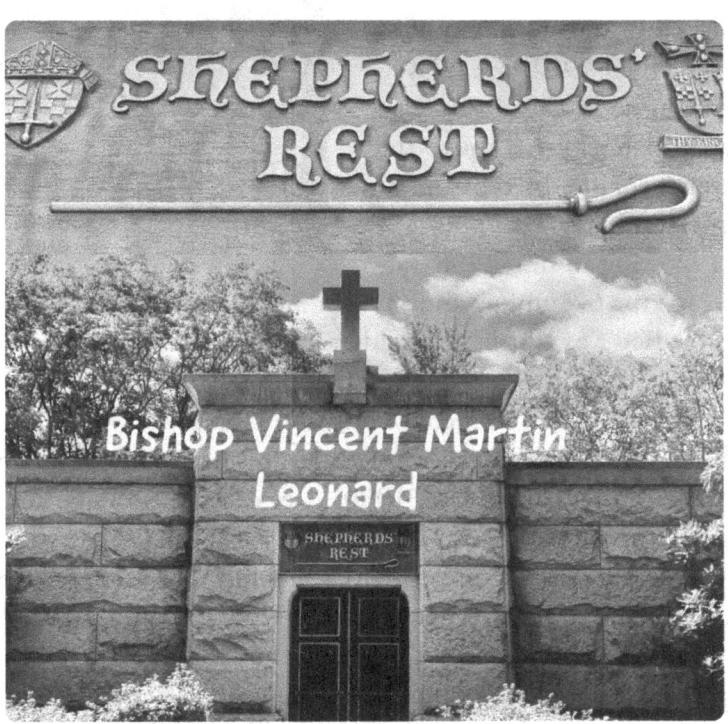

BILL REGAN

William Wright Regan was an American professional baseball second baseman. He played in the Majors (MLB) from 1926 to 1931 for the Boston Red Sox and Pittsburgh Pirates.

A native of Pittsburgh, Pennsylvania, Regan was a World War I veteran who played semi-pro baseball before starting his professional career in 1922. He played for teams in the Michigan-Ontario League and later moved on to the Columbus Senators of the American Association.

In 1925, Regan hit a .298 batting average for Columbus and .317 in 38 games in 1926, then joined the Boston Red Sox during the midseason to become the team's regular second baseman for the next five years. On June 16, 1928, he came to bat twice in an inning and homered both times. Sixty-two years later, Ellis Burks became the second player in Red Sox history to hit two home runs in the same inning (August 27, 1990). Regan was also Babe Ruth's last strikeout victim on September 28, 1930.

In 1929, Regan hit a career-high .288 while collecting 54 RBIs. He was still productive a year later, hitting 35 doubles and 10 triples. He played with the Pirates in 1931, his last primary league season.

Regan later played in the International League for the Baltimore Orioles, Buffalo Bisons, Montreal Royals, and Toronto Maple Leafs before ending his career in 1935 with the Birmingham Barons of the Southern League. While in Baltimore, he hit a career-high .321.

After retirement, Regan worked in the Allegheny County police department for 20 years and joined the armed forces during World War II.

Regan died in his hometown of Pittsburgh, Pennsylvania, at sixty-nine.

JULIUS JOSEPH "MOOSE" SOLTERS

Julius Joseph Solters was a major league outfielder between 1934 and 1943. Solters played nine seasons in the American League for four different teams: the Boston Red Sox (125 games), the St. Louis Browns (319 games), the Cleveland Indians (260 games), and the Chicago White Sox (234 games). During his major league career, he appeared in 938 games, batting .289 with 83 home runs and 599 RBIs.

On August 2, 1941, while playing for Chicago at Griffith Stadium in Washington DC, Solters was struck by an erratic baseball during a pregame warmup. The ball fractured his skull and contributed to him going blind two years later.

Julius Solters began his life in darkness and ended blind as well. He was born to Hungarian immigrant parents, and at a very early age, he worked leading mules in a coal mine near his home in Pittsburgh. He ended life without ever seeing his youngest son, Stevie, who was born after Solters lost his eyesight. He also may never have seen his older brother, John, who stayed behind when his parents came to America.

His father, Joseph George Solters, born in Homrogd, Hungary, worked as a coke puller for Jones & Laughlin steel company in Pittsburgh. The family struggled to get by, and young Julius worked several jobs, including grocery store clerk, baker's assistant, steel worker, sheet metal worker, ditch digger, truck driver, and coal miner. He set pins in a bowling alley during grade school. He always loved baseball. He was fortunate enough to have grown up near Forbes Field and shagged flies there as a young boy.

Julius went to Fifth Avenue High School for two years, but despite playing halfback on the football team, he could not stay interested in school and figured he was destined to become a laborer like his father.

Moose endured blindness for more than three decades, then suffered a stroke in February 1970 that debilitated him and forced him to redevelop his ability to speak. He learned Braille, read many books provided by the Library of Congress, and even helped host benefits to help others who have blindness. Five and a half years after his stroke, on September 28, 1975, he died in Pittsburgh.

Julius Joseph "Moose" Solters
ORIGINAL NAME Julius Soltesz
BIRTH 22 Mar 1906
Pittsburgh, Allegheny County, Pennsylvania, USA
DEATH 28 Sep 1975 (aged 69)
Pittsburgh, Allegheny County, Pennsylvania, USA

HERB DRURY

Herbert Joseph Drury was a Canadian-born American ice hockey defenseman who played for the Pittsburgh Pirates and Philadelphia Quakers for six seasons in the National Hockey League.

Drury began his hockey career with the Midland Seniors of the OHA senior league in 1914-15 and then moved to Port Colborne of the same league the following season. In 1916-17, he joined the Pittsburgh Yellow Jackets of the USA Hockey Association, where he stayed until 1924. He served in the US Army in 1918-19 and was granted US citizenship upon his honorable discharge from the military.

He played for the American National team at the 1920 Summer Olympics and the 1924 Winter Olympics, winning a silver medal both times. As a US Olympic hockey team member that competed in the first Winter Games in Chamonix, France, in 1924, Drury's US squad won its preliminary group, defeating Belgium 19-0, France 22-0, and Great Britain 11-0. In the medal round, they blanked Sweden 20-0 before losing 6-1 to Canada, and the U. S. won the silver medal. Drury scored an impressive 22 goals and three assists for 25 points in five games. He scored the only goal for the US in the gold medal game against his native Canada.

Following his retirement from hockey, Drury worked as a steamfitter in Pittsburgh and lived there until he died in 1965 at the age of seventy.

Herb Drury

JOSEPH A. McARDLE

Joseph A. McArdle was a member of the Democratic US House of Representatives for Pennsylvania. He served in the Pennsylvania State House of Representatives from 1936 to 1938.

McArdle was born in Muncie, Indiana, and moved to Pittsburgh with his parents in 1905. He attended parochial schools in Pittsburgh and worked in the insurance and bonding business.

McArdle was elected as a Democrat to the Seventy-sixth and Seventy-seventh Congresses and served until his resignation on January 5, 1942, to become a member of the Pittsburgh City Council.

He served as a Pittsburgh City Councilman until 1949. Also, in 1949, he switched parties to Republican and became the State GOP committeeman for Mount Washington, Pennsylvania, from early 1950 until 1966. On December 27, 1967, Joseph passed away in Pittsburgh.

JOHN B. "JACK" BUTLER

John Bradshaw Butler was born November 12, 1927, in South Oakland, Pittsburgh. Pennsylvania. Jack was an American football cornerback for the Pittsburgh Steelers in the National Football League.

Butler was an undrafted free agent who was signed to the Pittsburgh Steelers roster in 1951 out of St. Bonaventure. Steelers owner Art Rooney Sr. received a recommendation from his brother, Dan Rooney, a priest at St. Bonaventure, to look at Butler.

Known for his uncanny ability to find the football, Butler registered five interceptions during his rookie season. The following season, he led the Steelers with seven interceptions. In 1953, Butler had nine interceptions and recorded a record-tying four interceptions in one game against the Washington Redskins. Over the next nine NFL seasons, Butler proved himself as one of the game's most productive cornerbacks.

On occasions, Butler would play wide receiver for the Steelers. He scored a touchdown against the New York Giants. It was late in the game, and Butler caught a game-winning touchdown pass from quarterback Jim Finks.

During a game against the Philadelphia Eagles, Butler suffered a severe leg injury when he became tangled up with Eagles' tight end Pete Retzlaff. The injury forced Butler to retire in 1959.

In 103 games, Butler intercepted 52 passes, for which he returned 827 yards, and had four TD picks. He also had four touchdown receptions and returned one fumble recovery for a score.

Four Pro Bowls (1955-1959).

Four First-team All-Pro (1956-1959).

Interception titles (1952, 1953, 1956, 1957, 1958) NFL 1950's All-Decade Team.

Pittsburgh Steelers All-Time Team and Hall of Honor.

In 2012, Jack was elected to the Pro Football Hall of Fame.

Jack Butler died May 11, 2013, and was buried in the Calvary Catholic Cemetery in Pittsburgh.

PATRICIA DOBLER

Patricia Averdick was born in Middletown, Ohio, on June 18, 1939, and completed her BA in political science at St. Xavier College in Chicago. In 1961, she married writer Bruce Dobler. Bruce's career took them all over the United States before settling in Pittsburgh, where Pat began writing earnestly and earned her MFA at Pitt.

She is the author of *UXB* (Mill Hunk Books, 1991), Brittingham Prize in Poetry winner, *Talking to Strangers* (the University of Wisconsin Press, 1986), *Forget Your Life* (chapbook, the University of Nebraska Press), and *Now* (full-length collection).

Patricia's poems have appeared in such publications as *Mid-American Review*, *The Ohio Review*, *Ploughshares*, *Prairie Schooner*, and *Southern Poetry Review*.

Her work has been anthologized in *A Gathering of Poets*, *A New Geography of Poets*, *The Carnegie Mellon Anthology of Poetry*, *Working Classics*, *Vital Signs*, and *Anthology of Magazine Verse & Yearbook of American Poetry*, among others.

She received grants from the National Endowment for the Arts, the Pennsylvania Council on the Arts, fellowships from the Corporation of Yaddo and Villa Montalvo, and a Pushcart Poetry prize.

Patricia taught for many years at Carlow University, where she directed the Women's Creative Writing Center and the Madwomen in the Attic writing workshops.

Patricia died on July 24, 2004. Her Collected Poems were published by Autumn House Press in 2005 after her death.

REV. JAMES R. COX

Father James Renshaw Cox (1886–1951) was an American Roman Catholic priest in Pittsburgh, Pennsylvania, known for his pro-labor activism. He was a candidate for President of the United States in 1932 and organizer of an unprecedented protest march in Washington, DC.

Father Cox, from the Lawrenceville neighborhood of Pittsburgh, grew up during the industrial expansion. He began as a cab driver and steelworker, working through Duquesne University. He then entered Saint Vincent Seminary in Latrobe, Pennsylvania, and was ordained in 1911. From 1917 to 1919, he served in World War I as a chaplain at Base Hospital 27 at the Mongazon Seminary in Angers, France.

After the war, he enrolled at the University of Pittsburgh and earned a Master of Economics degree. In 1923, he was appointed pastor at the old St. Patrick Church in the Strip District.

During the Great Depression, he organized a food-relief program and helped the homeless and unemployed find shelter.

Known as the "Pastor of the Poor," he began a pro-labor march and led 25,000 people in Washington, DC, in 1932, forming the Jobless Party. At the time, it was the largest demonstration ever in the nation's capital.

After laying a wreath on the Unknown Soldier's tomb at Arlington, Father Cox and his army started on the 300-mile trip back to Pittsburgh.

Pennsylvania's most prosperous citizen, Secretary of the Treasury Andrew Mellon, paid the expenses for returning 276 stragglers by train.

Cox became the Jobless Party's candidate for President of the United States in 1932 before eventually withdrawing and supporting Franklin Roosevelt. The Jobless Party supported government public works and labor unions, spreading from Pittsburgh to other major cities.

GREGORY IGNATIUS ZATKOVICH

"The man who made himself president of a European Republic."

Gregory Ignatius Zatkovich was born in Galambos, Bereg County, Austria-Hungary (now Holubyne, Svaliava Raion, Zakarpattia Oblast, Ukraine) on December 2, 1886. At age five, he emigrated to Pennsylvania with his parents. His father, Pavel, was editor of the leading Rusyn-American newspaper.

Zatkovich graduated from high school in Pittsburgh, earned his undergraduate degree from the University of Pennsylvania in 1907, and his LL.D. from the law school at Penn in 1910. Soon after, he became a lawyer for General Motors in Pittsburgh.

In 1918, after four years of devastating war, the old order in Europe was about to collapse. Anticipating the tremendous political and social changes, Carpatho-Rusyns followed the example of other immigrant groups. They began to organize meetings to discuss the fate of their respective homelands. The most important of these meetings occurred on July 23, 1918, in Homestead, Pennsylvania, where the American National Council of the Uhro-Rusyns was formed. Within a few weeks, the council invited Zatkovich to serve as its spokesman in negotiations with the other ethnic groups and the United States government. They could not have made a better choice.

In October 1918, in Washington DC, the young Zatkovich met with President Woodrow Wilson and future Czechoslovak president Tomash

G. Masaryk. Then, in November, he led a Carpatho-Rusyn delegation to the Mid-European Union in Philadelphia. In Independence Hall, where America's Declaration of Independence was signed in 1776, Zatkovich and other Eastern European leaders signed a proclamation demanding independence for their people.

He was the first governor of Carpathian Ruthenia, the Rusyn autonomous province of Czechoslovakia, and the only American who was a governor of any territory that was or became part of the Soviet Union. However, his understanding of local autonomy was met with opposition from the Czechs, and within less than a year (March 21), he resigned from his post and returned to the United States. At first, he published several pamphlets attacking Czechoslovak policy in Subcarpathian Rus', but soon, he avoided immigrant politics and concentrated on his private law practice. He died on March 26, 1967.

ENOS KIRKPATRICK

Enos Claire Kirkpatrick went to college at Duquesne University in Pittsburgh. He played third base in the Major Leagues from 1912 through 1915. He was born December 9, 1884, and died April 14, 1964.

Kirkpatrick was the first major leaguer named Enos. Through the 2011 season, two other players with the same first name as Kirkpatrick played in the majors: Enos Slaughter and Enos Cabell.

Enos Kirkpatrick played two seasons in the National League and two in the Federal League. He played 97 games at third base, 29 games at shortstop, 27 games at second, 14 games at first, and a few games in the outfield.

A Sporting Life magazine article on March 15, 1913, reported Kirkpatrick's performance in spring training as excellent, which kept him in the majors after he hit under .200 the previous season. "The rejuvenation of Enos Kirkpatrick is a source of much joy among the elite here. . . . He has been getting his two or more hits per game and playing third base as though to the manor born, while his base-running has been far beyond expectations."

JOHN M. MORIN

John M. Morin was a congressional representative from Pennsylvania. Born in Philadelphia on April 18, 1868, he moved with his parents to Pittsburgh, where he attended the local schools.

In 1882, Morin started working at a glass factory and was later employed in the steel mills until 1885. He moved to Missoula, Montana, in 1889 and engaged in mercantile pursuits. During this time, he took a night course at Haskins' Business College at Missoula and graduated in 1892.

Returning to Pittsburgh, Morin engaged in the hotel business and became director of the Washington Trust Co. in 1910.

He was a member of the Pittsburgh Common Council from 1904 to 1906 and a delegate to the Republican state conventions from 1905 to 1912.

He became director of public safety in Pittsburgh from 1909 to 1913 and was elected as a Republican to the Sixty-third and the seven succeeding Congresses (March 4, 1913- March 3, 1929) as chairman.

He was on the Committee of Military Affairs (Sixty-ninth and Seventieth Congresses) and an unsuccessful candidate for renomination in 1928.

From 1928 until his death, he served as commissioner of the United States Employees' Compensation Commission in Washington, DC.

He died at the Marine Hospital in Baltimore, Maryland, on March 3, 1942.

JAMES FRANCES BURKE

James Burke was born in Petroleum Center, Pennsylvania, to Irish immigrants. Petroleum Center is listed as a populated place and ghost town in Venango County, Pennsylvania. In the 19th century, the name was also spelled "Petroleum Centre." The town of Petroleum Center flourished from 1865 to 1873, and its livelihood was in oil and entertainment. Today, it is nearly deserted.

James Burke studied law at the University of Michigan at Ann Arbor, where he graduated in 1892. While in school, he organized the American Republican College League, the predecessor to the College Republicans. Petitioning then-president Republican William McKinley, Burke won approval for the organization and hosted an inaugural banquet attended by McKinley, along with 1,500 college students. The organization quickly spread to almost every college in the country. In 1888, at age 21, Burke was made secretary of the committee in charge of the dedication of the new Allegheny County Court House, at which President Rutherford B. Hayes made the dedicating address.

After graduating from the University of Michigan, he was admitted to the Allegheny County bar.

Burke was then admitted to the Superior and Supreme Courts of Pennsylvania and later to the United States Supreme Court. Burke commenced his practice in Pittsburgh, Pennsylvania, and became the secretary of the Republican National Committee in 1892. That year, he resigned to devote his time to being president of the American Republican College League.

Burke was an avid golfer and belonged to several country clubs. He was the founder of the Beaumaris Yacht Club in Beaumaris, Ontario.

He was also a member of the exclusive Bath and Tennis Club in Palm Beach, Florida. At one point, the United States Golf Association asked him to prepare a set of rules, which was ultimately presented to the international committee at St. Andrews in Scotland.

In 1895, Burke married Josephine Birch Scott of Detroit, Michigan, and had two children, James Scott Burke and Josephine Frances Burke. He died in Washington, DC, and is buried at Calvary Cemetery.

JOHN KANE

John Kane was an American painter well known for his skill in Naïve art, a visual art created by a person lacking formal education and training. He was the first self-taught American painter in the 20th century to be recognized by a museum.

John Kane was born to Irish parents in West Calder, Scotland, on August 19, 1860. His father, employed as a grave digger in West Calder, would dig a grave on Friday and fill it on Monday. He died when John was 10, leaving behind a widow and seven children. Kane quit school to work at Young's Paraffin Works. During work, he was so struck with the malleability of the hot paraffin wax that he made a mask of his face for his mother, Biddy. He burned his face, but not too seriously. After his mother remarried, he emigrated to the United States at age 19, following his stepfather and older brother Patrick.

Kane worked for the Baltimore & Ohio Railroad in McKeesport as a gandy dancer who stamps down stones between the railroad ties. Next, he performed a stint in the steel industry at the National Tube Company in McKeesport but soon left for a job in Connellsville, Pennsylvania, at the coke ovens of Henry Clay Frick.

In the mid-1880s, Kane moved to mine coal in Alabama, Tennessee, and Kentucky. He then returned to western Pennsylvania, where he got other mining jobs to be closer to his family.

Kane started his new job painting steel railroad cars at the Pressed Steel Car Company in McKees Rocks, Pennsylvania. On his lunch hour, he began drawing on the side of railroad cars to "fill in the colors." He sketched landscapes on railroad cars instead of painting the required solid color. He tried to earn money for a short time by enlarging and tinting photographs for working-class families.

In 1925 and 1926, he submitted paintings to the Carnegie Internationals, which the Carnegie Museum of Art sponsored, but his works were rejected. The following year, Kane consulted Andrew Dasburg, who persuaded the jury to accept Kane's Scene in the Scottish Highlands (Carnegie Museum, Pittsburgh).

John Kane died of tuberculosis on August 10, 1934.

GERALD ANTHONY BUCCIARELLI

Gerald was born July 31, 1951, the eldest of three children. His younger sisters are Mary Lou Bruno and Josephine Grignon. His parents migrated to America from Italy's Abbruzzi region shortly after World War II. They settled in Pittsburgh, where his father worked in the steel mills and his mother, Marie, in a local department store. The family lived near Moore Park in Brookline, Pennsylvania. Jerry graduated from Resurrection Elementary School and South Hills Catholic High School (Class of 1969).

After graduating high school, Jerry moved to the West Coast, enrolling at Monterey Peninsula Junior College and later the University of California at Santa Cruz. This is where he discovered his passion, the theater. He formed his own company and then studied at the University of Washington and Temple University.

In 1976, Jerry moved to New York to seek employment. His stage name changed to Gerald Anthony. He took an off-Broadway directing job to make ends meet; then, in 1977, he accepted an offer for an eight-day stint playing a new character called Marco Dane in the daytime soap opera *One Life to Live*. His appearance would end up becoming a 17-year run playing that character. Marco Dane was rotten, and the fans loved him.

From 1981 to 1983, Jerry was married to actress Brynn Thayer, who co-starred as Jenny on *One Life to Live* from 1977-1986.

On May 28, 2004, at the age of 52, Anthony died by suicide in Butler, NJ.

JOHN J. KANE

John J. Kane, a state Representative from Allegheny County, was born in Pittsburgh, Allegheny County, Pennsylvania, on May 17, 1890. He attended Duquesne University and was the Pennsylvania representative for the International Printing Pressmen's Union of North America. In 1932, he was elected to the Pennsylvania House of Representatives as a Democrat. He resigned from the House on December 31, 1933. He was elected to the council of Pittsburgh (1934-1936). He was elected commissioner of Allegheny County from 1937-1960. He died on March 5, 1961, in New Brighton, Beaver County, PA, and was buried in Calvary Cemetery.

JUDGE WALTER R. LITTLE

Born in the South Side of Pittsburgh in 1943, Judge Walter R. Little, the youngest of 12 children, was raised by his mother in a public housing complex in the Hill District after his father died.

After graduating from Central Catholic High School, Walter Little served in the Army before earning an associate degree in 1968 from the Community College of Allegheny County. In 1970, he received a bachelor's degree from the University of Pittsburgh and a law degree from Pitt in 1973. In 1985, Little was elected to Common Pleas Court, where the tough stance he was known for continued in criminal court. A dedicated Catholic, he was part of a small group of prominent people who attended St. Benedict the Moor Church in Pittsburgh's Hill district.

Following a battle with prostate cancer, Walter R. Little died at the young age of 62 on June 5, 2006. Compounding the family's grief, the judge's brother, Anderson Little, 66, of the Hill, had died the day before, June 4. Anderson was the special projects director, executive producer, and host of the *Anderson Little Report*, a public affairs program on WDUQ-FM. The brothers are buried at Calvary Catholic Cemetery.

ANTHONY FAGNELLI

On June 23, 2021, Anthony, age 95, formerly of Oakland, was reunited with his late wife, Antoinette. He served 32 years as a Pittsburgh police officer. Anthony was a member of the Police Pistol Team and won several trophies.

Anthony was a renowned Graphoanalyst (handwriting analyst). He attributed his success predominantly to the in-depth studies of graphology. Handwriting analysis is virtually the only diagnostic method that can be used (retroactively) to evaluate the state of mind of a subject who is no longer alive or available to speak.

Anthony crafted his favorite subject with the science of handwriting in 1958. He was the past president of the Pennsylvania Chapter of the International Graphoanalysis Society of Chicago (IGAS). Anthony was recognized as one of the seven leading handwriting analysts in the United States. He was also praised for his study of Lee Harvey Oswald's writing.

There are red flags, warning signs, and caution signals in handwriting that place us on the alert that something is happening to a person. These happenings can be detected by observing the person's handwriting. Downhill writing indicates sadness, melancholy, and despair. This downhill writing is an initial indication of attitudes and feelings.

Some people write a little bit downhill all their lives but are never depressed. They are sad and tend to give a short insight into their emotions and how they unfold. To go further into the definition of downhill writing, a sagging "a" or "o" regarding the latter are warning signals of sadness and worry. The writer is having difficulty keeping their thoughts in a straight line—figure 2.

Lee Harvey Oswald dotted his letter "i" erratically. Oswald's failure to spot an "i" indicated he saw things that were not there. He was easily irritated and annoyed. Oswald would take a chance and risk a great deal, "a Gamble." There were never enough warnings to hold him back.

John Dillinger's handwriting shows one word trailing off into a long-stemmed ending.

James Earl Ray: The dominant factor was that many of his letters were broken. "Interrupted handwriting is rare and shows the thinking patterns are fragmented and disoriented."

The Boston Strangler, Albert De-Salvo, had misplaced letters in his writing. This shows a lapse of memory. He often wrote "bell" only to have it come out "behl."

Hitler's handwriting, by the early age of sixteen, was already to the extreme of going downhill. He maintained downhill writing throughout his life—figure 1. The writing will be level when we function well, free of melancholy and sadness. The writer maintains a remarkable ability to think.

Grandma Moses and Thomas Edison have a round top or flat top "m" and "n." This indicates creativity and dexterity.

Liberace has the same split writing as Beethoven and many famous musicians.

Figure 1: Hitler   *Figure 2: Drooping "o" and "a"*

From Jeanette Fagnelli (Argo), Anthony's daughter:

"My dad's accomplishments included being a member of the Pittsburgh Policemen Pistol Team and a Pittsburgh Police officer for 32 years. Prior to being a police officer, he was a baker at the Nabisco Company and worked on the assembly line for Dodge Automotive Company in Michigan. Dad served in WW2 United States Army in Germany. Some of the medals he received were the American Theater Ribbon and the Army Occupational Medal. Being a handwriting analyst, he wrote a book called *Teen Suicidal Tendencies as Revealed Through Handwriting*. Dad appeared in many other publications, including newspapers, television appearances, and radio interviews."

WILLIAM J. COYNE

William Joseph Coyne (August 24, 1936 – November 3, 2013) was a Democratic member of the United States House of Representatives from Pennsylvania from 1981 to 2003. From 1970 to 1972, he was a member of the Pennsylvania House of Representatives; he was a member of the Pennsylvania House of Representatives and a member of the Pittsburgh City Council from 1974 to 1980. Coyne was elected to Congress in 1980, succeeding 24-year incumbent William S. Moorhead in a district taking in most of Pittsburgh. He was reelected ten times, never facing serious opposition. He was a longtime member of the United States House Committee on Ways and Means and represented that committee for five years on the House Budget Committee. He also served on the House Banking Committee, the Committee on House Administration, and the Committee on Standards of Official Conduct, known unofficially as the House Ethics Committee.

A few of his accomplishments are listed: making permanent the federal Industrial Revenue Bond program, which gives tax breaks to older cities to rebuild their manufacturing bases; expanding the earned income tax credit and ensuring that it is paid monthly to low-income working Americans; and securing pro-consumer reforms at the Internal Revenue Service.

Coyne also steered millions of dollars to the 14th District for local programs—from redeveloping the Hays Munitions Plant to constructing a new building for Children's Hospital to ensuring that Pittsburgh was

included in a federal study of infant mortality. Other successes include $2 million to set up the NASA Robotics Engineering Consortium and $14 million for the Sawmill Run flood control project.

ISTVÁN (STEPHEN) KEREKES

A letter from Ms. Boglarka Kis.

This is my grandmother's grandfather. His name is István (Stephen) Kerekes. He arrived at Ellis Island on May 7, 1907, on a ship called *Ryndam* from Rotterdam, The Netherlands.

He came with almost nothing, but he was a very hard-working man. He had a family back in Hungary, but unfortunately, they were never brave enough for this long journey. Nevertheless, he supported his family throughout his life and achieved a lot in his new homeland.

He was successful, created a good existence for himself, and gave work to many people. He also had the chance to visit his family before he died in 1934 and meet my grandmother (his grandchild) in his hometown. After his death, his son traveled to Pittsburgh to sell his legacy.

I attached a picture of the grave and another one of my great-great-grandfather.

Dear Ed,

I cannot express how much it means to me that you fixed this grave.

This means that the grave will remain, and the life of this man will not pass without a trace.

In the meantime, we arrived back in Hungary. If you are planning to visit Budapest, please let me know; it would be a pleasure to show you the city or invite you for dinner.

Thank you again, and God bless you!

Kind regards,
Bogi

LOCAL BURIALS

My dad, **J. Roy Murray**, was in the mill with the Feds during the war. He was President of Local #1843, Hazelwood, J&L Steel. He served in the tank corps at Ft. Knox.

Sharyn Haddock:
My grandfather, **Patrick Haddock,** is there. He built Pitt Stadium and Western Psychiatric. My father built the Fort Pitt tunnels and the downtown Pittsburgh YWCA.

Tom Lysaught: "Michael Thomas Lysaught"

One of Pittsburgh's great athletes, Lysaught, was a veteran of World War I, a former football player at Duquesne University, and a member of the old Lafayette professional basketball team before and after WWI. He was also a professional boxer, singer, and actor. He also composed more than 80 songs, many of which were published.

Michael Lysaught is buried with Agnes Eliz.

OUR BABIES

The Final Resting Place

INFANT NEW SECTION

RELIGIOUS SISTERS

CLERGY

THOU ART A PRIEST
FOR

THE FORGOTTEN

THE LEGENDS, THE HEROES

The Legends, the Heroes

Private George P. Toner (Tomer) Mustered into service August 22, 1862 Company E 155 Pa. Infantry. Discharged on surgeon's certificate, date unknown.

Arthur Lemon, Company C. First Sergeant

Private William J. Barry mustered into service January 1, 1864. Mustered out with Company D 76 PA. Infantry on July 18, 1865, Vet.

76TH PA. INFANTRY

The 76th Volunteer Infantry Regimental Flag is the "Keystone Zouaves." The regiment was organized during the fall of 1861 and detached on July 18, 1865. The infantry comprised men from Lawrence, Mercer, Blair, York, Snyder, Bedford, Westmorland, Indian, Luzerne, Dauphin, Allegheny, Beaver, and Schuylkill Counties.

The 76th was organized at Harrisburg, Pennsylvania, under the command of Colonel John M. Power. The regiment was attached to the Department of the South.

The 19th U. S. Infantry was organized by the direction of the President on May 4, 1861, and confirmed by an Act of Congress on July 29, 1861. Then, it was reorganized in Indianapolis and ordered to Kentucky in October 1861. They were then attached to Rousseau's Brigade, McCook's Command, at Nolin, KY, Army of the Ohio, to November 1861.

The 19th United States Infantry Regiment lost three officers and 55 enlisted men, killed and mortally wounded, and two officers and 124 enlisted men to disease in the Civil War. Most of its service was in the Western Theater, but Companies G and H were detached in the East for part of the war.

Nickname: "The Rock of Chickamauga" (special designation)
Motto: The Rock of Chickamauga

The 62nd was organized at Pittsburgh, Pennsylvania, beginning July 4, 1861, and disbanded on August 31, 1861. The Volunteer Infantry

Regimental Flag is the same as the 76th. The Regiments 51 to 100 incorporate the same flag. The 62nd was under the command of Colonel Samuel W. Black. Companies L and M were transferred to the 91st Pennsylvania Infantry, and the veterans and recruits were transferred to the 155th Pennsylvania Infantry.

The 155th Pennsylvania Volunteer Infantry Regiment served in the Army of the Potomac in the Eastern Theater battle. The 155th Regimental flag was designed for the men from Allegheny, Westmorland, Clarion, and Armstrong Counties. The regiment was organized in the fall of 1862 and was detached from service on June 2, 1865.

155 PA INFANTRY

155 PA Infantry

INDEPENDENCE DAY

THE PAUPER GRAVES

LIGHT SHINING DOWN

The Final Resting Place

Light Shining Down 113

William F. Houck 1940–1941

Joe Stanchina
Died February 22, 1956

Daugherty
Baby John 3rd
Born—March 28, 1957
Died—July 22, 1057

RANDOM BEAUTY

Random Beauty

The Final Resting Place

CALVARY CEMETERY MAP

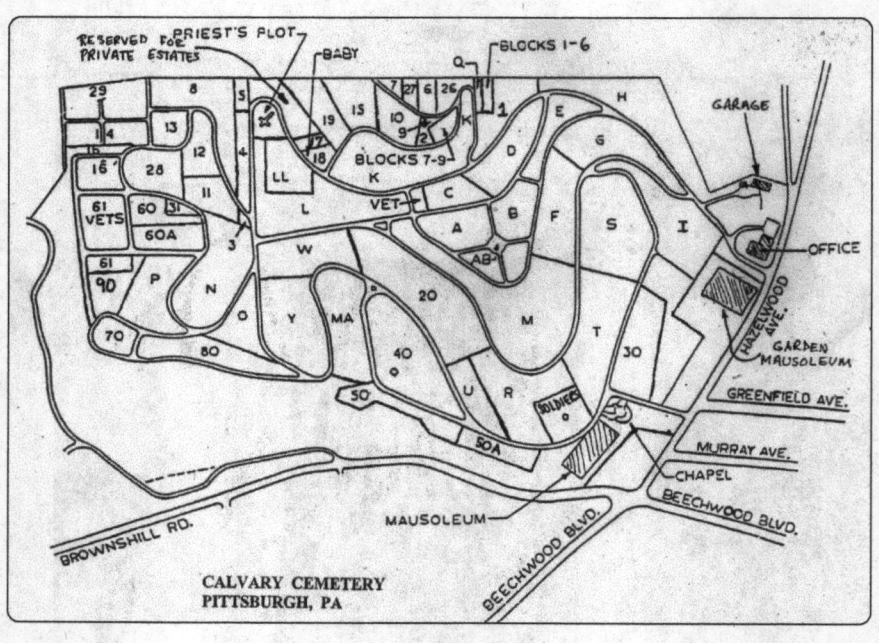

BIDDLE NEWSPAPER ARTICLE

From *The Evening Tribune* (San Diego, California), Saturday, February 1, 1909:

CAUGHT THE CONVICTS AFTER A FATAL FIGHT

The Warden Declares That He Was Under the Influence of Chloroform When Prisoners Made Their Escape

Associated Press Special Leased Wire.

Butler, Pa, Feb. 1—The condition this morning of the fugitives from justice, the Biddle brothers and Mrs. Soffel who were wounded in the battle with the Pittsburg and Butler police, last evening, had not changed since midnight, except in the case of Edward Biddle, who has grown weaker and who has almost continual internal hemorrhage. Mrs. Soffel's only wound was made by a bullet which penetrated the left breast. It was from a 32-calibre revolver and coursed around the rib to the left side, lodging in the shoulder blade. Dr. McAdoo operated on her, removing the bullet and her recovery is probable. Mrs. Soffel tells two stories of the shooting, one that she shot herself during the fight, and the other that she was shot by Edward Biddle. The bullet did not go through her outer garment which indicates that the shot was fired by herself or by Biddle by putting the hand under the coat.

JACK BIDDLE'S STORY

From the statement made this morning by Jack Biddle in his cell, it is evident that the escaped convicts and their accomplice had arranged to commit suicide in case capture became imminent. In addition, Jack also told how they escaped. Their manner of getting out of jail, according to his statement, was the same as has already been published. McGeary, he says, fell over the railing when he jerked loose from the hold the prisoner had on him. He says Mrs. Soffel helped effect, and officers are now on their way to this place to take back the prisoners at any cost. Doctors Green and Bricker, who have been attending the two Biddles, made a report this morning that apparently confirms Jack Biddle's story that the fugitives had tried to kill themselves. They had come to this conclusion after a complete examination and a partial probing of the wounds of both men. Ed Biddle, who is generally supposed to be the worst injured, has several powder marks on his left breast which would go to show that he attempted to kill himself. In Jack's mouth are three bullet wounds, which would be prima facie evidence that he wanted to rid the world of himself. One of the bullets, which evidently came from a revolver, carried away a portion of his tonsil, which, the doctors say, could only have happened by the holding of a revolver to his own mouth. One of his other wounds is through his abdomen and it is thought into his bowels, and this may cause his death. Bullets from two of his other wounds about the stomach were taken out this morning.

About 10:30 this morning Mrs. Soffel took a bad turn and her condition is more serious. She asked for her children and they will probably be sent for. Edward Biddle is unconscious and breathing heavily. His death may occur at any moment. John Biddle has recovered from the opiates administered and talks in a boastful strain. The doctors now say that while he may live several days his ultimate recovery is deemed impossible.

EXCITEMENT AT BUTLER

There is great excitement in the town and the streets are crowded, large

ed them to escape but would not say she supplied the saws. The sawing of the bars of the cells, he says, was completed before January 14th and several times previous to the day on which the escape was made their plans failed through some little detail.

Jack again reiterated that he never killed anyone and that he never put a bullet into anyone except Keeper Reynolds. He said the first crime he ever committed was assisting to rob a liquor store at Carnegie but admitted that he had participated in a number of robberies after that. After they had left the jail they went to a house near a railroad in Pittsburg. They remained all of Thursday. The people in the house, when they read of the escape from the jail, recognized them and would only let them remain after the Biddles gave them a "bunch of money."

They remained at the house until Thursday night leaving it as soon as it grew dark. Jack says he wanted to stay there, and that Ed also was willing to stay, but that "the woman was nervous and afraid they would be caught."

"I would not let them go alone," Jack said, "and as soon as it grew dark we went down the street took a street car. We rode to the end of the line and then walked until we reached the farm where we stole the horse. If it had not been for the woman we would not have been caught, for we could easily have gotten another horse and by this time been more than 100 miles away. Its a lead pipe cinch that we would have escaped but we could not let that poor woman go by herself. She did all she could with us—betrayed her husband, deserted her family all to help us out—and we would have been a great deal worse than we are thought to be if we had thrown her down.

"When we saw the officers coming toward us on the road yesterday evening we knew it was all up. We did not fire a shot at the officers, but attempted to kill ourselves. I shot myself in the mouth. Ed shot himself over the heart and the woman shot herself in the breast. We knew we had no chance to get away and we knew we would swing if taken back, and that is why we wanted to kill ourselves.

WERE SHOT MANY TIMES

The Biddles when captured, had on the same clothes they wore when they escaped. Jack, had in addition, a light overcoat. Mrs. Soffel also had on the clothes in which she left her home. Through Edward's coat there is one bullet hole, but through the dark velvet vest he wore are two holes that lodged near his heart. Jack's coat and vest are literally riddled. There are four holes in the side of the coat and ten in the right sleeve. The latter appear to have been made by small bullets. Jack's pistol was a cheap 32-calibre affair. Three of the six chambers of the gun hold empty cartridges. Both of the Biddles were talkative this morning but both disclaimed ever having killed any one.

numbers surrounding the hospital. A conflict between the Pittsburg and Butler authorities over the possession of the prisoners and the right to the reward is confidently expected. The Butler authorities assert that they will not give up the prisoners without a writ of habeas corpus.

District Attorney John C. Haymaker left for Butler at 10:45 this morning over the Pittsburg and Western railroad. He stated that he did not think he would have any difficulty in straightening out the tangle at Butler, and also said he was of the opinion that if it was at all feasible the Biddles would be removed to this city at the earliest possible moment. Much depended, he said, on what condition the prisoners were in and that he could not say definitely as to what action he could take until he had investigated for himself.

The declaration by Edward Biddle that he did not shoot Detective Fitzgerald and was not implicated in the Khaney murder is given no credence by the superintendent of police and Kelly.

As to the Biddle's declaration that neither of them was at the Khaney house the night of the murder, Detective Kelly said: "That is absurd. Fred Ohlinger positively identified them as did several others. The Zebers woman was accounted for that night. The Biddles statement in this regard is absurd, as a preponderance of evidence shows."

Fromer Warden Soffel made the startling statement that he had been under the influence of chloroform when the prisoners got away. The warden believes the opiate was administered by his wife. The Butler officers demand half the reward of $5000 and in order to hold the prisoners, warrants were sworn out for Biddles, charging them with felonious shooting in attempting to kill Mrs. Soffel.

District Attorney Haymaker, says the position taken by the Butler officials is wholly untenable, and steps will be taken at once to compel them to relinquish their claims.

As there is nothing to hold Mrs. Soffel as a prisoner, Mr. Haymaker will prefer charges against her of felonious assault and battery and aid and assisting a prisoner to escape from a place of confinement.

PROBABLY ALL WILL DIE

Butler, Pa., Feb. 1—1:20 p. m. The Biddles are believed to be dying, and Mrs. Soffel has developed pneumonia and her condition is more serious than ever.

THE STORM CONTINUES

London, Feb. 1—The storm in the English and Irish channels is unabated. Numerous minor wrecks have occurred, frequent reports have been received of men washed overboard and the crews of the life boats and rocket apparatus have been kept busy. The British armored cruiser Immortallte encountered terrific weather.

The Khaney murder, Ed alleged, was committed by Walter Dorman, assisted by a man who had that day come from Chicago, and the Zebers woman, who put on a man's suit. This Ed says she had often done before when she had assisted them in their robberies. He admitted having committed a great many robberies, but stoutly maintained that he had never killed anyone.

THEIR CONDITION

Dr. Bricker is in constant attendance at the cells of the Biddles. He says their wounds will not permit of their being removed and feels certain that a journey to Pittsburg today would be sure death to Ed Biddle. Notwithstanding this, however, it is the intention of the Pittsburg authorities to have them moved to Pittsburg at once, regardless of consequences. Supt. of Police Demmel has wired here to that

The seas washed clean over her 9.2 inch forward guns.

Many fishermen are reported to have been drowned. In the Clyde upwards of forty vessels are fog-bound between Greenock and Glasgow.

The mail steamer which left Dover for Ostend yesterday afternoon was sighted in distress in the channel this morning. Tugs assisted her into port. Her passengers had terrible experiences The steamer was swept by the seas for over 20 hours.

BOND PURCHASE TO CONTINUE

Washington, Feb. 1—Secretary Shaw of the treasury department today stated for the present at least he would continue the purchase of bonds for the sinking fund on the present basis.

Mrs. Kate Soffel

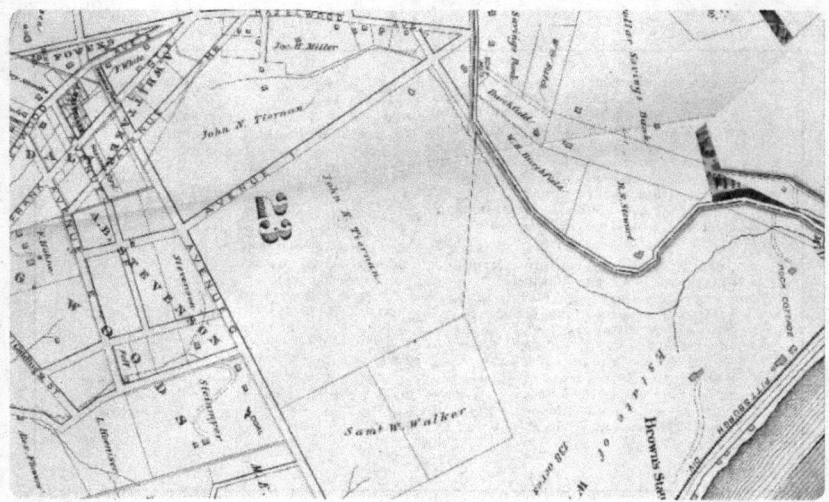

1882

Peebles 1862

PLACING FLAGS FOR MEMORIAL DAY

The Final Resting Place

ACKNOWLEDGMENTS

This book has evolved through the input of many people. I thank the Calvary Catholic Cemetery employees Elaine Savko, Marcy Shotts, Kelly Stephens, Ashley Boehm, Charlotte Levis, John Smouse, Lauren Sanker, Lyndsy Garrett, Rick Richert, and Tyler Smith.

Thanks to Judeen Wayman for the information on Tom Lysaught. Judeen's Uncle first over.

Thank you, Linda Webster, "Minuteman Press owner," Gary Timlin, and Jeanette Fagnelli (Argo).

Thanks to Robert Houck for the knowledge and location of the "Paupers Grave" site. The people back in the woods need to be recognized.

Thanks to Pietrzak Gilbert for the photos and the Pittsburgh Carnegie Library.

Finally, my wife, Anna Marie Bonner, for her support and advice.

ABOUT THE AUTHOR

EDWARD BONNER is an author with a passion for poetry as well as historical works. His published works include:

Ed grew up in a small steel mill town called Hazelwood Pittsburgh, Pennsylvania.

In addition, he has had a lifelong passion for the martial arts. He has competed in numerous tournaments and placed often in regional and national competitions. He also owned his karate school in his current hometown of Canonsburg, Pennsylvania.

Ed's educational background includes Catholic and public education as well as a degree in business and Aeronautics.

He was employed by US Airways/American Airlines for over thirty-two years.

Ed has been an athlete all his life by competing in triathlons, 5k runs, college, and McKeesport Daily News baseball. He has been active in coaching children in sports.

Ed has been married to his wife, Anna Marie, for thirty-six years. They are the proud parents of two adult children, Brooke and Patrick. With their spouses, he is blessed with four grandchildren.

Ed has participated in All Poetry as a host and competition for his writings. And continues to read at coffee houses and libraries.

www.ingramcontent.com/pod-product-compliance
Lightning Source LLC
Chambersburg PA
CBHW010856090426
42737CB00019B/3384